Up, Up and Away
Monarch Butterflies

by Marta Magellan
Illustrations by Mauro Magellan
Photos by James Gersing

Eifrig Publishing LLC
Lemont | Berlin

Science Editor

Deanne Endrizzi
Wildlife biologist of the
U.S. Fish and Wildlife Services

Education Editor

Katie-Lyn Bunney
Education Manager, Monarch Joint Venture

Photographs by

James Gersing

Dedication

As always,
to Sammy Joe Schnall,
who loved leaves, balloons, and yellow

Monarch butterfly
Lindsey Lambert

Monarch butterflies are nature's wonder.

Legend has it that early settlers to North America admired the monarch's bright orange color. It made them think of Prince William of Orange who became a king. So they gave the butterfly the name monarch, which means ruler or king.

Monarchs are many people's favorite butterfly. They are the most studied, tracked, and recognized of all butterflies.

What makes them the celebrities of the insect world?

Monarch butterflies go on a big adventure every year.

Many millions take to the skies when it begins to get chilly in the northern United States and southern Canada. It is an awesome sight. They are flying south to a sunny place, but they're not going on vacation. Cold winters will kill them.

This kind of journey is called migration. They don't use maps or GPS like we do, but they know which way to go. They use the position of the sun and the earth's magnetic fields to find their way.

But monarchs aren't the only butterflies who migrate.

So why are they such a big deal?

Monarchs are the only butterflies who make a two-way flight.

Like birds, they fly south for the winter and head north when the weather gets warm.

The western monarchs fly to coastal California. The eastern monarchs tackle a much longer trip. They fly all the way to Central Mexico. It takes them about two months along a path called a flyway.

In Mexico, they cluster together for months on oyamel fir trees.

Yet, when spring comes around, they don't live long enough to make it back.

Aren't they supposed to be round-trip flyers?

The egg-to-butterfly life cycle

Egg (hatches in about 4 days), **caterpillar or larva** (this stage lasts 9-14 days), **chrysalis or pupa** (this stage lasts 10 to 12 days), **adult butterfly** (lives two or three weeks, except the super generation which lives 8-9 months).

Monarchs go through several life cycles to finish the trip.

To get back up north, it takes them three or four generations. A **generation** is a group of living things born around the same time. The generation that flies thousands of miles to California or Mexico lives eight to nine months. It is called the **super generation**. On the way back, they only have a few weeks left to live.

To complete the journey, they lay eggs and go through their entire life cycle three or four times during the trip. The last generation ends up in the same spot their great-great-grandparents, the super generation, came from. They had never been there before.

How did the great-great-grandchildren know where to go?

Migrating monarchs use instinct.

That means they are born knowing what to do. It's like they have a secret code in their brains guiding them. Instinct tells each generation things like how to travel along the flyway using the position of the sun. Instinct shows them how to lay eggs only on plants called milkweeds. It also leads them back to the birthplace of their great-great grandparents.

But sometimes, new buildings or farms take over fields of wildflowers. The milkweeds and flowers from the year before may be gone.

Can their instincts help them?

Monarch butterflies' instincts drive them to adapt.

That means that to survive, they must find plants with nectar. They will look around for places where flowers and milkweeds might still grow, like parks and gardens.

But little by little, their **habitats** have been disappearing. **Habitats** are the fields of wildflowers monarchs need to survive. There are more buildings and more farms now. So every season, we might see fewer monarchs along the flyway.

But wait. We see monarchs all around us.  Or do we?

The Look-Alikes

Viceroy butterfly

Soldier butterfly

Passion butterfly (Gulf fritillary)

Queen butterfly

They might be monarch copycats.

Some butterflies sport the exact same colors and even similar patterns. Look at the pictures of the look-alike butterflies. They can fool you into thinking they're monarchs.

What are these imposters up to?

The monarch's bright colors are a warning to birds and frogs. "If you eat me, you'll be sorry!" Birds throw up if they gobble up a monarch. And they will learn a lesson. No more orange butterflies for them. Monarch colors are like a special shield announcing they carry poison in their bodies. They taste terrible to birds and frogs.

It's easy for people to think the look-alikes mimic or copy the monarchs to stay safe.

But do they?

The monarch isn't the only butterfly that carries poisons.

Monarch butterflies only lay eggs on milkweed plants. Milkweed has poison. When caterpillars hatch, they munch on it. The chemicals stay in their bodies even as adults.

But guess what? All the look-alike butterflies also lay eggs on plants that have chemicals. They taste as bad as the monarchs. By looking alike, they all stay safe, so don't feel bad if you can't tell which is which.

That's the point.

One butterfly *will* fool you, though. It looks exactly like the migrating monarch people watch for every season.

But it isn't one. Not exactly.

Monarch butterfly laying eggs

Resident monarch sipping nectar from tropical milkweed

It's a monarch that doesn't migrate.

All over the world there are resident monarchs. That means they live in one place and don't travel far. Florida is one of the few places in the United States where almost all monarchs are residents. Who doesn't like year-round sunshine, right?

But there's something else.

Milkweed.

A type called scarlet or tropical milkweed grows all over Florida and some southern states. Monarchs lay their eggs on it and caterpillars eat it all year long.

These monarchs can't migrate.

They can't or they won't?

Monarchs used to migrate in Florida.

For a long time, only native milkweeds grew. Native milkweeds, like butterfly weed and swamp milkweed, died every fall. So monarchs left town, too.

When the monarchs returned, they found new milkweed growing back, clean of parasites.

Parasites are tiny, single cell organisms that live off other living things. Monarchs can get sick from them.

When tropical milkweed arrived in Florida, things changed. It doesn't die back every fall. Tropical milkweed hangs around all year, so parasites do, too.

But those parasites have been around a long time.

So what's the problem?

Monarch caterpillar on tropical milkweed

Monarchs may get too sick to fly.

Caterpillars emerge from the eggs and eat leaves full of parasite spores. The caterpillars grow into infected adult butterflies. Sick monarchs are sometimes born with crumpled wings and die. Many do live, but their wings are weaker. They can't fly long distances, so they cannot migrate. If they live, they don't fly far. They become residents.

What's wrong with staying in one place?

Some people think tropical milkweed is fine. It helps keep monarchs alive, so they keep planting it. But most scientists say monarchs infected with parasites are a problem. They don't live as long, they mate less, and they lay eggs at the wrong time. Their flying ability isn't too good, either.

And sick resident monarchs pose a danger to migrant monarchs. If infected butterflies meet migrating monarchs, they pass on parasites to them. Few of us want the migrants to lose their ability to migrate.

But is it all the tropical milkweed's fault?

Resident monarch on tropical milkweed

Migrant monarchs run into many troubles.

Every year people watch for the spectacular appearance of the monarchs when they take to the skies. Those migrants are not endangered. But they are at risk.

Too many chemicals used to kill bugs from gardens and crops also kill butterflies. Other chemicals to kill weeds also kill the flowers butterflies need for nectar.

When people need new buildings, they sometimes destroy fields with wildflowers.

Climate change makes the weather unpredictable.

All those infected butterflies fluttering around can't be helping.

Are the migrating monarchs doomed?

Monarchs are not doomed. Not yet.

There are still plenty of monarchs to watch, but you can help keep it that way.

Start by planting a butterfly garden. By growing what monarchs and all butterflies need to survive, you will help nature do its job.

You can become a **citizen scientist**. With your parents, you can help scientists collect information about monarch butterflies right where you live. You and all the other community scientists can keep track of the magnificent migrating monarchs.

And you'll have fun doing it.

How great is that?

Become a citizen scientist.

Journey North engages citizen scientists from across North America in tracking migration and seasonal change. Volunteers submit observations of the first monarchs in the spring, roosts in the fall, as well as first emergence and presence of milkweed. Website: journeynorth.org/monarchs.

Project Monarch Health is a community science project working to track the protozoan parasite OE in monarch butterflies in North America. Anyone can participate, people of all skills, ages, and backgrounds, classrooms, organizations, etc. Website: monarchparasites.org/

iNaturalist has projects that identify and catalog milkweeds in the United States. Several organizations such as Florida Nature Trackers and the National Park Services work with iNaturalist. Website: inaturalist.org/

Monarch Joint Venture is a partnership between government, businesses, schools, and organizations, working together to protect the monarch migration across the United States. See opportunities for community scientists to help in monarch conservation, from planting habitat to educating others. Website: monarchjointventure.org/

Turn the page for the best way to
plant your butterfly garden.

Plant a Butterfly Garden

If you live along the flyway...

- To provide a habitat for migrating monarchs, plant your own butterfly garden along the sunny side of a garage or a solid fence

- Start with at least two kinds of native milkweeds as host plants so monarchs have somewhere to lay their eggs.

- Add some native flowering plants so that butterflies have nectar to keep them going on their long trip. Flowers will help not just monarchs, but other butterflies, insects, and hummingbirds also. Let them share.

- Ask your parents to avoid using pesticides, like those called systemic pesticides. They kill insects you may not like, but they also kill the good insects.

- Pull the weeds out by hand and avoid weed killers like glyphosate (Roundup).

Butterfly weed — Deanne Nendrizzi

If you live in Florida:

- Replace tropical milkweed with native milkweeds. Make sure to pull out the tropical milkweed by the roots.

- In South Florida, there are already enough milkweeds for the many resident monarchs. Help the butterflies that are in serious trouble like the Florida Leafwing and the Atala hairstreak by planting pine croton or coontie.

- Ask your parents to keep chemicals (pesticides and weed killers) out of your yard and garden. Those are very harmful to bees and butterflies (not good for humans, either).

If you don't have a yard...

- Work with your community, such as libraries or neighborhood organizations of all kinds to create habitats for monarchs and other pollinators.

- At school, you can ask teachers or the principal to help you start a butterfly garden. Tell them it's a learning opportunity.

- If you have a balcony or patio, plant nectar flowers in containers.

For everyone:

Never rear captive butterflies to release them into the wild. They will spread even more parasites that way. Let nature do its job.

Glossary and Brainy Vocabulary

Danaus plexippus: monarch butterfly's scientific name

Flyway: the paths and routes birds and butterflies use on their migration journeys

Generation: a group of animals (including butterflies and people) born and living at or around the same time.

Instinct: a skill animals are born knowing how to do, like baby ducks following their mother

Migrate/Migration: when animals move from one place to another at certain times of year in search of food, water, or warm weather.

Mimicry: in biology, a way unrelated organisms copy each other so that predators leave them alone.

   Batesian Mimicry: the harmless one copies the colors of the dangerous one

   Müllerian Mimicry: the look-alike dangerous ones mutually benefit from their similar appearance, such as monarch butterflies and viceroy butterflies

Ophryocystis elektroscirrha: scientific name for the protozoan parasite that affects monarch butterflies, called OE for short

Spores: tiny seed-like parts of the parasites that cling to milkweed and infect monarch butterflies

Selected References

Bittel, Jason. (4 Oct. 2023) "Monarch butterflies aren't endangered, reversing recent decision. Is that good news?" National Geographic.

Clement, K. and Crawford P.H. C. (Dec. 2020) "Fall available tropical milkweed (Aclepias curassavica L.) may be a population sink for the monarch butterfly. Oklahoma Native Plant Record. https://ojs.library.okstate.edu/osu/index.

Davis, Andrew K and J. C. de Roode. (13 Dec. 2018) "Effects of the parasite, Ophryocystis elektroscirrha, on wing characteristics important for migration in the monarch butterfly." Animal Migration. De Gruyer Open Access. https://doi.org/10.1515/ami-2018-0008.

Goulson, Dave. 2021. Silent Earth: Averting the Insect Apocalypse. Pp 54-55. HarperCollins Publishers New York.

National Park Service. (updated 15 August, 2021) "NETN Species Spotlight: Monarch Butterflies." 12 March 2019. https://www.nps.gov./articles-spotlight-monarchs

Satterfield, D, Maerz, J.and Altizer, (22 Feb. 2015) S. Loss of migratory behaviour increases infection risk for butterfly host. The Royal Society Publishing. https://doi.org/10.1098/rspb.2014.1734

U.S. Fish and Wildlife Service (USFW). 1 Sept. 2020. Accessed 12 Jul 2023. "Monarch Butterfly Species Status Assessment (SSA) Report.

Acknowledgments

Thank you to Cathy Snyder, who sparked the creation of the garden helper series of books. Her hospitality and her passion for educating children on the importance of pollinators has been invaluable. Also grateful to Marilyn Smith, of the Sisterhood of the Traveling Plants, and the St. Augustine Garden Club and its generous volunteers.

To publisher Penny Eifrig, for her belief in books and in the importance of wildlife and sustainability.

For manuscript critique, my 12X12 nonfiction critique group, Jaclyn Boice, Songju Daemicke, Christine Iverson, and Kimberly Marcus; SCBWI critique group members, Lisa Wilcke, Patricia Morissey, Kristi Lozano; Marc Magellan and Jennifer McDevitt.

A shout-out goes to Tamian Wood for her beautiful designs of this and many of our books.

My deepest gratitude for everything goes to my children, Tracy Monique and Marc Gabriel, to my best friend, James, and to my cherished grandchildren.

©2024 Marta Magellan
Printed in the United States of America

All rights reserved. This publication is protected by Copyright, and permission should be obtained from the publisher prior to any prohibited reproduction, storage in a retrieval system, or transmission in any form or by any means, electronic, mechanical, photocopying, recording, or likewise.

Published by Eifrig Publishing,
Lemont, PA | Berlin, Germany.
For information regarding permission, write to:
Rights and Permissions Department, Eifrig Publishing,
PO Box 66, Lemont, PA 16851, USA.
permissions@eifrigpublishing.com, +1-888-340-6543

Library of Congress Cataloging-in-Publication Data
Up, Up and Away Monarch Butterflies/
by Marta Magellan
p. cm.
Paperback: ISBN 978-1-63233-386-5 | Hardcover: ISBN 978-1-63233-387-2 | eBook: ISBN 978-1-63233-388-9
1. Nature - Juvenile Nonfiction. 2. butterflies, insects, pollinators, milkweed, parasites - Juvenile Nonfiction
I. Magellan, Mauro, ill. II. Title
28 27 26 25 2024
5 4 3 2 1

Cover & book design by Tamian Wood www.BeyondDesignBooks.com
Illustrations by Mauro Magellan | Photos by James Gersing
Printed on recycled PCW acid-free paper

About the Author and Illustrator

Marta Magellan and Mauro Magellan are a brother and sister author/illustrator team who now work together after having published separately for many years.

You can learn more about both author and illustrator at: www.martamagellan.com

www.ingramcontent.com/pod-product-compliance
Lightning Source LLC
Chambersburg PA
CBHW041602070526
44586CB00003BA/54